T0021530

NATIONAL
GEOGRAPHIC
KiDS

# Brother, Sister, Me and You

Mary Quattlebaum

NATIONAL GEOGRAPHIC
WASHINGTON, D.C.

Sister lion leaps

and pounces.

Honeybees
do
wiggle-bounces.

Ducklings paddle

through the water.

7

# Brother
splashes sister otter.

Turtle babies

push through sand.

11

# Robins flap and gently land.

Beavers build

14

a lodge with sticks.

15

Guppies flash with finny flicks.

Bear cubs tumble, climb, explore.

Wolf pups snuggle, softly snore.

Lion, turtle, bouncing bee ...

brother, sister, you and me.

23

Play, swim, splash, creep ...

build, bounce, flap, sleep.

Brother, sister,
me and you ...

these are things that we do, too!

27

## Afterword
### by Tovah P. Klein, Ph.D.

**The sibling bond is like no other.** I call it a "lab for later" because brothers and sisters help each other develop skills and strengths to handle life's ups and downs. They figure out how to solve problems and handle conflict. They learn about love as they form a uniquely intimate bond. Siblings discover what it means to look out for others, to share in each other's joy, and to be there when the going gets tough.

Just as the animals in *Brother, Sister, Me and You* pounce and prod, snuggle and scuffle, human siblings play and squabble, giggle and wrestle, too. They share family, upbringing, and experiences in the same household. Older siblings protect younger ones; younger ones look up to big brothers and sisters as role models. They share sibling secrets, create family rituals, and wink at common jokes.

Siblings also share the most prized people in their lives—their parents. This is where complications evolve, so the sibling bond is naturally accompanied by jealousy. Siblings vie for parental attention and affection. And just as the bear cubs in this book have to find room to climb onto Mama Bear, so children have to make room for each other with their parents.

Parents worry about the intensity of their children's conflicts—from jealousy of a new baby to physical fighting and harsh words for each other—even as they marvel at the love and connection between their children. These clashes of conflicts and love, rivalries and tenderness are to be expected. In the warmth and trust of sibling bonds, children get to be themselves, in all their feelings and behaviors. Their bond allows them to test the limits and to know that even at their worst moments, they can come back and have their brother or sister at their side.

So what is a parent to do when siblings go from laughing one moment to fighting the next? The best advice I can give is to hold back as best you can, to be on the sidelines and to intervene only when you feel that safety is an issue. Let your children know that it can be hard to have a brother or sister, and that sometimes they might need a break from each other.

It is impossible to be an impartial judge to your own children. When left to their own, without direct parent intervention, siblings usually resolve conflicts and return to play because the conflict is based in a relationship of love and companionship. It's important to let children have their relationship, with all its negatives and positives, pouncing and prodding, nudging and snuggling. When parents step back and give their children the space to do this, the sibling relationship deepens into a strong bond that brothers and sisters carry throughout life.

28

# Animal Facts

**Animals often have brothers and sisters, just as humans do.** Some animal siblings play together, others merely share a nest or birthplace. Some live together as adults, others go their separate ways as soon as they are born or hatched. Some animal siblings work together to complete a task. Others even care for younger siblings.

Like human sisters and brothers, certain types of animal siblings play, pounce, wrestle, and snuggle together. Many scientists believe that these activities help them learn to hunt, protect themselves, strengthen family bonds, and cooperate with larger groups when they are grown. These behaviors may also help prepare them to be parents.

## Lion

Lions live in Africa and parts of Asia. Lion mothers give birth to one to four cubs. Cubs like to play and often stalk and pounce on one another. These games may help prepare them for their adult roles as hunters (females) and protectors (males). Lions live in large family groups called prides. A pride usually has two to three males and several females and their cubs. At the age of two, males leave the pride, but females stay and become hunters. Mothers, daughters, and sisters work together to bring down large prey such as wildebeests, zebras, impalas, and warthogs. The young males sometimes travel and hunt together as they search for a new pride to join.

## Honeybee

Honeybees are native to Africa, Europe, and Asia, but they have been introduced throughout the world. These social insects live in groups called colonies, in nests called hives. Each colony has one queen bee. She lays thousands of eggs. Her female offspring become worker bees. Worker bees collect nectar and pollen from flowers. When a worker bee returns to the hive, it sometimes does a bouncy "waggle dance" that shows other workers where to find the flowers. The worker bees make honey from the nectar.

# Mallard Duck

Mallard ducks are found in ponds, lakes, and wetlands in Asia, Europe, and North America. A female mallard builds a nest of twigs and feathers close to the ground and lays one to 13 eggs in it. After hatching, the ducklings can swim and feed themselves within 24 hours. They stay close to their mother for protection. They swim when she swims, and they nestle under her body to sleep. When they are about two months old, they fly off on their own.

# Eurasian Otter

Eurasian otters live near rivers, lakes, streams, and coastlines in parts of Europe, Asia, and Africa. A mother otter gives birth to two or three kits, also called pups or cubs. The kits begin to swim at about two months old. They dive, splash, tumble, and chase one another. Playing helps the kits learn how to hunt the fish, clams, birds, and insects they will eat when they stop drinking their mother's milk. Otters stay with their mother until they are 14 months old.

# Leatherback Sea Turtle

Leatherback sea turtles live in the Atlantic, Pacific, and Indian Oceans, and the Mediterranean Sea. Females swim thousands of miles between feeding grounds and nesting sites. A mother turtle leaves the water at night, digs a nest on the beach, lays about 100 eggs, covers them with sand, and returns to the sea. The eggs hatch in two months, and the hatchlings push through the sand with their flippers. They move quickly to the sea, often in a group.

# European Robin

European robins are found in parts of Europe, Africa, and Asia. A mother robin lays four to six red-speckled eggs. Both parents care for the chicks. At two weeks old, the fledglings leave the nest and flutter to the ground. Their parents continue to feed them for a few weeks, until the young robins learn to find their own worms, berries, and insects, and their wings grow strong enough to fly. American robins look similar and behave much the same, but they are a different kind of bird. They lay blue eggs.

# Beaver

Beavers are found across North America, Europe, and Asia in ponds, rivers, lakes, and swamps. Beavers build their lodge, or home, from branches, twigs, and mud. They live in family groups called colonies. A beaver mother has three to five babies, called kits, at a time. Both parents care for the kits. The kits' older brothers and sisters also help care for and play with them. The young beavers romp, dive, and splash with their broad, flat tails. They also help repair the family's lodge and build dams.

# Guppy

Guppies live in the wild in rivers and lakes in South America. They are popular pets, too. In the wild, guppies eat algae and brine shrimp. Most fish lay eggs, but a female guppy gives birth to live babies—sometimes as many as 200 within a few hours. These baby fish, called fry, can swim and eat as soon as they are born. Guppies are social fish. They enjoy being in groups, called shoals, or swimming together in schools.

# Brown Bear

Brown bears live in Europe, Asia, and North America. In the winter, a mother bear gives birth in a den, usually to two cubs. The tiny cubs drink milk from their mother and stay close to her for warmth. When spring comes, the bears leave the den. Now the cubs are big enough to play, wrestle, climb, and explore together under their mother's watchful eye. They learn to find berries, roots, insects, fish, and small mammals to eat. The cubs stay with their mother for two to three years.

# Gray Wolf

Gray wolves live in parts of North America and Asia. Wolf mothers have litters of four to six pups. Wolves live in family groups called packs, which usually include the parents, their offspring, aunts, and uncles. The parents are in charge. The whole pack, including older siblings, helps to care for the pups by bringing them food, watching over them, and teaching them to hunt. Pups wrestle, chase, pounce, and play tugging games with one another. They snuggle and lick faces to show affection.

*To Helen, Mel, Paul, Ann, Linda, and Danny—*
with happy memories of all the pouncing, bouncing,
splashing, and exploring we did as kids —*MQ*

Text Copyright © 2019 Mary Quattlebaum
Compilation Copyright © 2019 National Geographic Partners, LLC.
All rights reserved.

Published by National Geographic Partners, LLC, Washington, D.C. 20036.
All rights reserved. Reproduction of the whole or any part of the contents
without written permission from the publisher is prohibited.

NATIONAL GEOGRAPHIC and Yellow Border Design are trademarks
of the National Geographic Society, used under license.

Designed by Amanda Larsen

Library of Congress Cataloging-in-Publication Data

Names: Quattlebaum, Mary, author.
Title: Brother, sister, me and you / by Mary Quattlebaum.
Description: Washington, DC : National Geographic Kids, [2018] |
  Audience: Age: 2-5. | Audience: Pre-school, excluding K.
Identifiers: LCCN 2018026409| ISBN 9781426332906 (hardcover) |
  ISBN 9781426332913 (hardcover)
Subjects: LCSH: Brothers and sisters--Juvenile literature. |
  Animals--Juvenile literature. | Familial behavior in animals--Juvenile
  literature.
Classification: LCC BF723.S43 Q38 2018 | DDC 306.875--dc23
LC record available at https://lccn.loc.gov/2018026409

Printed in China
18/PPS/1

**CREDITS**
Cover, Denis-Huot/Nature Picture Library; back cover, J.-L. Klein
& M.-L. Hubert; front flap, Shutterstock; back flap, (author),
Michelle Rivet; (consultant), Carol Weinberg; 1, Paul Hobson/
Nature Picture Library; 2-3, Albie Venter/NiS/Minden Pictures;
4, Eric Tourneret/Biosphoto; 5, irin-k/Shutterstock; 6-7, Vicki
Jauron, Babylon and Beyond Photography/Moment/Getty
Images; 8, Eric Isselee/Shutterstock; 9, Arco Images GmbH/
Alamy Stock Photo; 10-11, Jurgen Freund/Nature Picture Library;
12, John Daniels/ARDEA; 13, idp wildlife collection/Alamy Stock
Photo; 14-15, Robert McGouey/Wildlife/Alamy Stock Photo; 16,
Gerard Lacz/FLPA/Minden Pictures; 17, SOMMAI/Shutterstock;
18-19, Suzi Eszterhas/Minden Pictures; 20, Lisa & Mike Husar/
Team Husar; 21, Klein and Hubert/Minden Pictures; 22, Yva
Momatiuk and John Eastcott/Minden Pictures; 23, Donald Iain
Smith/Moment/Getty Images; 24 (LO LE), Mike Powell/The
Image Bank/Getty Images; 24 (UP LE), Inti St Clair/Blend
Images/Getty Images; 24 (LO RT), Chris Stein/The Image Bank/
Getty Images; 24 (UP RT), Melodious Vision/The Image Bank/
Getty Images; 25 (UP RT), Ariel Skelley/Blend Images/Getty
Images; 25 (LO), Ascent Xmedia/The Image Bank/Getty
Images; 25 (UP LE), Sue Barr/Image Source/Getty Images;
26-27, Big Cheese Photo LLC/Alamy Stock Photo; 28, Eric
Isselee/Shutterstock; 28 (UP RT), irin-k/Shutterstock; 28 (LO),
SOMMAI/Shutterstock; 29 (UP), Albie Venter/NiS/Minden
Pictures; 29 (LO), Eric Tourneret/Biosphoto; 30 (UP), Vicki Jauron,
Babylon and Beyond Photography/Moment/Getty Images; 30
(UP CTR), Arco Images GmbH/Alamy Stock Photo; 30 (LO CTR),
Jurgen Freund/Nature Picture Library; 30 (LO), John Daniels/
ARDEA; 31 (UP), Robert McGouey/Wildlife/Alamy Stock Photo;
31 (UP CTR), Gerard Lacz/FLPA/Minden Pictures; 31 (LO CTR),
Suzi Eszterhas/Minden Pictures; 31 (LO), Klein and Hubert/
Minden Pictures